C000001039

Fleeting Shadows

How **Christ** transforms the darkness

CWR

Malcolm Duncan

For Mum and Dad Hunter.
The shadows aren't forever.

In memory of John Kendall.

Contents

Acknowledgements

My deep appreciation goes to Lynette and the team at CWR. Thank you so much for your patience and your enthusiasm for this little book. In what has been an incredibly unpredictable and difficult time, your understanding and support has been wonderful.

Thank you also to the family at Gold Hill. I love you so very much and thank God for you. What a privilege to be part of this church community.

My thanks, as always, to my Personal Assistant, Maria Bond. Your tireless support means so much to me. At the time of writing you are facing your dark shadow of loss. May God continue to comfort you.

Of course my thanks go to my wife Deborah, and my four children, Matthew, Benjamin, Anna and Riodhna. Thank you for your love and support. You are inspirational.

Lastly, my deepest and most profound thanks go to the Lord Jesus Christ, whose light and life have given me meaning and purpose. May You be glorified through these words and may many be drawn to You.

Soli Deo Gloria

Introduction

Sometimes the darkness in our lives is very threatening.

This Lent study guide is aimed at helping you to reflect on some of the ways in which life can be engulfed in uncertainty or darkness. My prayer is that God will use it across this Lenten period to draw you close to Him and to remind you that no matter how dark things might seem, God is closer than you think.

The idea for the book was born out of what has been an incredibly difficult year for me. I speak more about that in Study Four, so I will leave you to read the details there. Suffice to say there have been times over the last eighteen months when I have felt the darkness of death and sadness of despair very personally and very deeply. My faith has been through a profound period of testing and growth. I love God more than I have ever loved Him, but I understand Him less than I have ever understood Him. I have to say, though, I trust Him more now than I have ever done and my faith has become even more simple and straightforward. At its heart, my conviction is simple – God is good, and His mercy endures forever. He is near the brokenhearted and close to those who mourn. I hold onto that with all my heart.

Shadows come to us in many forms. There is the worry of today, the sheer exhaustion of trying to keep too many plates spinning, the need to make choices that are right and honouring to God, the pain of death and despair, facing our demons and confronting our insecurities and anxiousness about the future. These subjects form the six studies that are before you. I am aware that there are many other shadows that we face. Shadows of depression, or calamity or disaster or doubt, but the reality is that this is a simple guide aimed at helping you draw near to God as He draws near to you. It is not a depressing book. Instead it is a book full of hope, confidence and faith; but I hope authentic hope, authentic confidence and authentic faith.

I've shared some of my own stories in the book, mostly stories of failure, mistakes and struggles. That doesn't mean that these are the only aspects of my life that exist – far from it.

I am simply trying to be authentic, open and honest. My faith is still growing. I still struggle with God. I don't have all the answers and I have not tried to write a self-help guide.

As we approach Holy Week, I invite you to be vulnerable enough to think about areas in your life and your faith where you need to be reminded of God's grace and love; power and faithfulness. I invite you to be honest. I invite you to confront the shadows in your life. I do so, however, with the strong conviction that all the shadows we face are fleeting. The great light of the resurrected King Jesus will one day dispel every cloud, remove every shadow and chase away every fear. Many of the shadows in our lives lurk with intent, but God is stronger than they are. With this guide we will explore the words of Psalm 23 coupled with some of the 'I am' sayings of Christ found in John's Gospel. Read them slowly and allow them to sink in. Take time to let God's Word live in you and produce life in you and through you. Please use the prayers, reflections and other material I have included here as you see fit.

A few years ago I was driving along the A40 between Oxford and Burford and was caught in the most beautiful sunrise. That stretch of road is always beautiful, but on that particular morning it was simply spectacular. I stopped the car, stepped outside and enjoyed the morning sun as it spilled across the fields. The light bounced off the crops like shimmering diamonds. All around me the darkness, which just moments before had been shrouding the earth, released its grip. It scurried away as the light tumbled out from its source so many millions of miles away. The sky glowed red with anticipation and the world looked different. The sun had got its hat on and was coming out to play!

I love sunrises. They fill me with hope. They are a daily reminder from God that light is stronger than darkness. They are utterly dependable and predictable, and they serve as jaw-droppingly beautiful memos from heaven, with hope written all over them. Sunrises force shadows to flee. They push back the chill of the darkness and they call the earth out of slumber. They are a wake-up call to creation. They are also an optical illusion. Of course the sun does not revolve around us, we revolve around it. We just think the sun revolves around us and use language that betrays our egocentricity as a race and a planet.

In the same way, our Son has risen. He does not pander to our needs, He does not jump to our tune. He stands resplendent in light and alive in power, grace and tenderness. His presence is guaranteed and when the shadows see Him, they flee. We just sometimes don't believe it. We sometimes think it is too good to be true. We sometimes prefer the darkness to the light. May God change our perspective.

May the shadows be dispelled by hope.

May God draw close to you as you prepare for Holy Week and the message of God's deep unshakeable love for you.

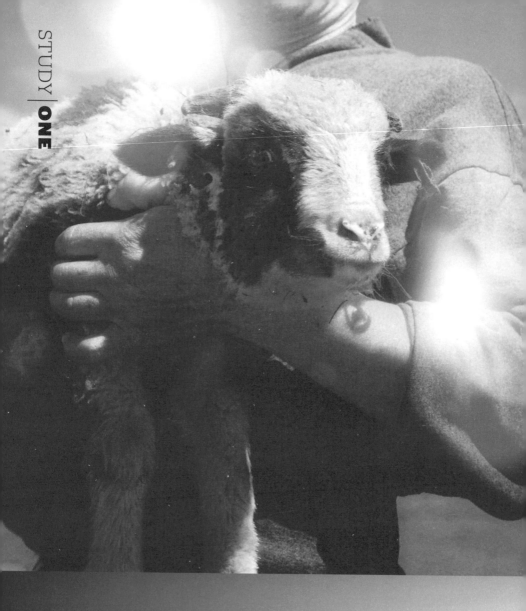

Our Shepherd in the Shadow of Today

Psalm 23:1; John 10:11-16

Warm Up

Take a blank sheet of paper and write down twenty ways in which the Lord has provided for you or protected you in the last month. Please do not repeat anything on the list. What is the impact of making this list on your thinking and attitude?

Opening Prayer

Father, thank You that You are always present with us. Would You come close to us as we embark on this most holy subject. Remind us of how much You love us and how willing You are to protect us, nurture us and provide for us. Help us lift our gaze to You so that we discover again the joy of Your work in our lives. Amen.

Eye Opener

Sometimes the pressures of living leave us feeling like we are always living under a cloud. We can get caught in the vice-like grip of traps like developing our careers, paying the bills or keeping up appearances. When this happens, we discover that no matter how much we have, it never seems to be enough. As the dark shadows of discontent fall across the landscape of our lives we end up worrying about what we do not have rather than being thankful for what we do have. Yet when God is our shepherd, we lack nothing. What does that mean?

Setting the Scene

The two central passages we are reflecting on in this first study are the opening verse of Psalm 23 and Jesus' self-identification as the Good Shepherd in John 10:11–16.

The idea of God as our shepherd is one of the most important images in the Bible. Throughout the Scriptures, we have pictures of God as the shepherd of Israel and Jesus as the shepherd of all who follow Him. In one of the most beautiful passages about God's loving care and commitment to those who have gone astray (Luke 15), Jesus paints a picture of God as a shepherd who goes out of His way to find the sheep that has wandered.

Deeply embedded in the metaphor of God as our shepherd is the reality that shepherds are important figures in the Middle East. Throughout the years, they have been central to the wellbeing of their flocks and to the wellbeing of their whole communities. The shepherd is a protector and a provider. The shepherd leads the sheep. When one of the sheep is hurt, the shepherd will go and get them and make sure that they remain with the rest of the flock.

As you read through these scriptures do so very slowly, allowing the imagery to really come to life in your imagination.

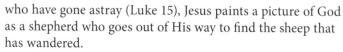 Bible Readings

Psalm 23:1
'The LORD is my shepherd, I lack nothing.'

John 10:11–16
'I am the good shepherd. The good shepherd lays down his life for the sheep. The hired hand is not the shepherd and does not own the sheep. So when he sees the wolf coming, he abandons the sheep and runs away. Then the wolf attacks the flock and scatters it. The man runs away because he is a hired hand and cares nothing for the sheep.

I am the good shepherd; I know my sheep and my sheep know me – just as the Father knows me and I know the Father – and I lay down my life for the sheep. I have other sheep that are not of this sheepfold. I must bring them also. They too will listen to my voice, and there shall be one flock and one shepherd.'

Luke 15:3–7
'Then Jesus told them this parable: "Suppose one of you has a hundred sheep and loses one of them. Doesn't he leave the ninety-nine in the open country and go after the lost sheep until he finds it? And when he finds it, he

joyfully puts it on his shoulders and goes home. Then
he calls his friends and neighbours together and says,
'Rejoice with me; I have found my lost sheep.' I tell you
that in the same way there will be more rejoicing in
heaven over one sinner who repents than over ninety-nine
righteous people who do not need to repent.'"

Psalm 95:6–7
'Come, let us bow down in worship,
let us kneel before the LORD our Maker;
for he is our God
and we are the people of his pasture,
the flock under his care.'

Isaiah 40:11
'He tends his flock like a shepherd:
he gathers the lambs in his arms
and carries them close to his heart;
he gently leads those that have young.'

1 Peter 5:4
'And when the Chief Shepherd appears, you will receive
the crown of glory that will never fade away.'

Revelation 7:16–17
'"Never again will they hunger;
never again will they thirst.
The sun will not beat down on them,"
nor any scorching heat.
For the Lamb at the centre of the throne
will be their shepherd;
"he will lead them to springs of living water."
"And God will wipe away every tear from their eyes.'"

Hebrews 13:20–21
'Now may the God of peace, who through the blood of the
eternal covenant brought back from the dead our Lord

Jesus, that great Shepherd of the sheep, equip you with everything good for doing his will, and may he work in us what is pleasing to him, through Jesus Christ, to whom be glory for ever and ever. Amen.'

Session Focus

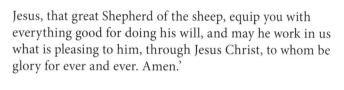

Life can be harsh and unrelenting. I have been a Christian since 1986 and I am still learning to trust God with the day-to-day challenges of life. If there is such a thing as an expert in faith, it certainly isn't me. There are still days when I struggle to make it through and I wonder where God is. When I lived in Scotland in the early 1990s, there were days when my wife and I had nothing to eat and no money to buy electricity or gas. They were days when our faith was tested very deeply. I felt like a failure as a husband and as a Christian. It is hard to be joyful when you do not know where the next meal is coming from.

Yet as time has gone on, I have discovered an ever-deepening sense of this simple reality, God will not abandon me. Even when I *feel* like He is *not* there, I have an ever-strengthening *sense of conviction* that He is *always* there. In the words of C.S. Lewis, 'I believe in Christianity as I believe that the sun has risen: not only because I see it, but because by it I see everything else.' Today I believe God is my shepherd more than I have ever believed it. That does not mean I find it easy to trust God, it just means I am learning what it means to take Him at His word.

It is because God is my shepherd that I can be assured that He will provide everything I need (Psa. 23:1). He is a shepherd who provides for His sheep, who protects His sheep and who is utterly committed to His sheep. His provision for us is not simply about physical food and drink because there can be no doubt that Christians still go hungry in the world today. Only a Christian who lives in the largely prosperous northern hemisphere could equate God's shepherding of His people with nothing more than physical food and drink. The idea of God being our shepherd *is* about such provision, but it is about much, much more than that too.

As our shepherd, God is the source of our protection, our hope and our strength. Sheep in the Middle East are at the mercy of the wild when they leave the safety of the sheep pen. The only thing between them and the wild animals that want to destroy them is the shepherd who has their best interests at heart. Put simply, without the presence of the shepherd, the sheep have no hope. The same is true of us as followers of Christ.

Jesus told His disciples that He is the Good Shepherd (John 10:11–16). He is not simply *a* good shepherd, He is *the* Good Shepherd. He protects us. He nurtures us. He guides us. He shields us. He looks for us when we wander away from Him. He rescues us from the darkness of our own mistakes. He snatches us from the impending danger of attacks around us. Jesus as our Good Shepherd sacrifices Himself for our security. He puts His own life on the line so that our lives can be saved. He does not only bring us the offer of security, He *Himself* is our security.

The Early Church held this idea of Jesus as their shepherd as a central part of their faith in Him. Peter describes Jesus as our 'Chief Shepherd' (1 Pet. 5:4) and when John records his visions of Jesus in the book of Revelation, he describes seeing a Lamb who has become a gentle but strong and loving shepherd (Rev. 7:16–17). The earliest images of Jesus, found in the catacombs in Rome, picture Him as a shepherd who carries His lambs gently.

What kind of shepherd is Jesus to us? He is One who knows us. He understands our frailty and gently lifts us and carries us in His arm. He holds us close to His heart and shields us from danger (Isa. 40:11).

Whatever happens today, it is not out of sight of the Good Shepherd. He loves us too much to abandon us. He is always there and He always will be. Just because you cannot always see Him, does not mean that He cannot always see you.

Discussion Starters

1. When have you found it hard to trust God and what was it that caused you to wonder whether God was with you?

2. Do you find trusting God easy or hard? Why do you think that is?

3. ~~Look again at the list you made at the beginning of~~ this ~~study.~~ How does remembering God's goodness to you in the past help you with the present?

4. How do you address the reality that there are Christians in the world at this moment who are hungry and without shelter? What could you or your church family do to help?

5. Do you know someone who is currently finding it hard to trust God? How could you or your Christian friends help them?

_____

_____

_____

_____

6. What do you think are some of the causes of a lack of trust in God's provision and how would you address those issues?

_____

_____

_____

_____

7. Look at Psalm 23:1 again. Is there an area in your life where you feel you are lacking in some way? Take a few moments to lay that specific issue before the Lord in prayer.

_____

_____

_____

_____

8. Read John 10:11–16 aloud. What specific truths can you find in those verses? Hold onto them this week.

_____

_____

_____

_____

Final Thoughts

The times when I have found it hardest to trust God are the times when I have been most disappointed with what is happening in my life. If I am not careful, I allow my circumstances to become the lens through which I view God instead of allowing God to be the lens through which I view my circumstances. Learning to trust that God has my best interests at heart is hard when things seem to be going wrong. In those moments, one of the things that helps me most is a deliberate choice to remember that I know the end of the story of my life – God wins!

The anxieties of the present can rob us of the joy that flows from knowing that God, in the end, will put all things right. The inevitable tensions of living in a broken world do not change the promises that God has made His people. He will wipe every tear from our eyes. We will enjoy the continual experience of His presence, grace and power in our lives. Keeping this perspective strengthens our faith and gives us courage to keep going when things are difficult.

Closing Prayer

God my shepherd,
I focus my eyes on You.
I lift to You the issues that concern me today …
I lift to You the people for whom I carry a burden …
Please help me to trust You anew.
Let me see Your provision and Your nearness in new ways.
Remind me of Your faithfulness and kindness.
Amen.

Further Reflection

Each day this week, take a few moments to read John 10:11–17 and Psalm 23:1. Try to memorise these Scriptures if you can. Each day for the next seven days record the new insights that God gives you on these truths and fashion those insights into prayers of thanksgiving.

Our Restorer in the Shadow of Exhaustion

Psalm 23:2-3; John 10:7-10

Warm Up

Take a few minutes to make a list of all the things that you have done in the last week. How many people have you seen and what things did you talk about or achieve? Do you often feel tired by the end of the week or not?

Opening Prayer

Father, thank You that You have promised to give rest and refreshment to Your people. Would You draw near to us by the power of the Holy Spirit and remind us of Your deep grace and unfailing love. Refresh and renew us as we spend time reflecting on Your character and Your commitment to us, Your people. Give us strength, faith and courage to serve You. Amen.

Eye Opener

Running on empty sometimes feels like the normal state of affairs but it can feel like we are sinking and there's no one to save us. For many people, rest has become a luxury that they no longer feel able to afford. It doesn't take long before the strain begins to show and our lives become disordered. The symptoms of our malaise are easy to spot: irritability, loss of concentration, an absence of enjoyment in things that we used to really look forward to are just a few. What do you do when you have no energy left to do anything?

Setting the Scene

There are three central sections of Scripture for us to reflect on in this second study: Psalm 23:2–3, John 10:7–10, where Jesus tells His disciples that He is the gate, and Matthew 11:28–30, where Jesus invites all those who are weary and burdened with heavy loads to come to Him and find rest for their souls.

The passages before us remind us of the deep peace and strengthening that is to be found in a relationship with God. So often we end up allowing our relationship with God to become very utilitarian. By that I mean we come to Him because He does things for us. Our relationship with Him ends up feeling more like a transaction. That is not how God wants it to be. He longs for a relationship of deep trust and joy with us, one in which we love Him for who He is, not just what He does for us.

As we read through the scriptures set out here, we are confronted with two very powerful realities. The first is that God gives a promise of His provision of rest, care and sustenance. This is an absolute guarantee from God. He will restore those who come to Him. The second is that He will not force us to come to Him. Restoration is assured but entering it and enjoying it is an invitation to which we are asked to respond.

Bible Readings

Psalm 23:2–3
'He makes me lie down in green pastures,
he leads me beside quiet waters,
he refreshes my soul.'

John 10:7–10
'Therefore Jesus said again, "Very truly I tell you, I am the gate for the sheep. All who have come before me are thieves and robbers, but the sheep have not listened to them. I am the gate; whoever enters through me will be saved. They will come in and go out, and find pasture. The thief comes only to steal and kill and destroy; I have come that they may have life, and have it to the full."'

Matthew 11:28–30
'Come to me, all you who are weary and burdened, and I will give you rest. Take my yoke upon you and learn from me, for I am gentle and humble in heart, and you will find rest for your souls. For my yoke is easy and my burden is light.'

Isaiah 14:30
'The poorest of the poor will find pasture,
and the needy will lie down in safety.'

Ezekiel 34:11–16
'For this is what the Sovereign LORD says: I myself will
search for my sheep and look after them. As a shepherd
looks after his scattered flock when he is with them, so will
I look after my sheep. I will rescue them from all the places
where they were scattered on a day of clouds and darkness.
I will bring them out from the nations and gather them
from the countries, and I will bring them into their own
land. I will pasture them on the mountains of Israel, in the
ravines and in all the settlements in the land. I will tend
them in a good pasture, and the mountain heights of Israel
will be their grazing land. There they will lie down in good
grazing land, and there they will feed in a rich pasture on
the mountains of Israel. I myself will tend my sheep and
make them lie down, declares the Sovereign LORD. I will
search for the lost and bring back the strays. I will bind up
the injured and strengthen the weak, but the sleek and the
strong I will destroy. I will shepherd the flock with justice.'

Psalm 62:1–2,5–8
'Truly my soul finds rest in God;
my salvation comes from him.
Truly he is my rock and my salvation;
he is my fortress, I shall never be shaken ...
Yes, my soul, find rest in God;
my hope comes from him.
Truly he is my rock and my salvation;
he is my fortress, I shall not be shaken.
My salvation and my honour depend on God;
he is my mighty rock, my refuge.
Trust in him at all times, you people;
pour out your hearts to him,
for God is our refuge.'

1 Peter 5:10–11
'And the God of all grace, who called you to his eternal
glory in Christ, after you have suffered a little while,
will himself restore you and make you strong, firm and
steadfast. To him be the power for ever and ever. Amen.'

Session Focus

Sometimes we have no choice but to rest. In 1991 I was one of
the volunteers at Billy Graham's 'Mission Scotland' event. It
was an exciting and exhausting time. As well as volunteering
to work through the night on each evening of the campaign, I
was helping to plant a church and working in a full-time job.
After three weeks I collapsed with exhaustion. In my zeal I
was burning the candle at both ends and in the middle. My
exhaustion was caused by my own bad judgment. My recovery
was a gift of His grace.

Psalm 23:2 reminds us that God 'causes' or 'makes' us
lie down in green pastures and leads us beside quiet waters.
The imagery is laden with beautiful messages of stillness,
restfulness and restoration. Green pastures speak to us of
comfortable spaces, fresh food and uninterrupted peace. Quiet
waters remind us of God's promise to restore, refresh and
renew us.

One of the great challenges of modern living is the tendency
we have to rush around all the time. We sometimes think we are
indispensable. This flawed understanding of our own importance
feeds the wrong part of our self-understanding. We love to be
needed, but if we are not careful we end up taking our identity and
value from what we do instead of who we are. God does not want
it to be this way. He does not want His people living in a constant
state of exhaustion and collapse. Exhaustion causes us to live with
dark and wrong views of ourselves and of our place in the world.
Its effects can be bad for our health physically, emotionally and
psychologically. God longs to refresh and renew us and to give us
His strength and power on a continual basis.

Jesus tells His disciples that He is the gateway or the entry point to good pasture (John 10:7–10). He reminds His disciples that His offer of relationship is not one that leads to more and more burdens and expectations being placed upon them, but instead leads to a better and more balanced life. Eugene Peterson captures this beautifully in his paraphrase of Matthew 11:28–30 in *The Message*: 'Are you tired? Worn out? Burned out on religion? Come to me. Get away with me and you'll recover your life. I'll show you how to take a real rest. Walk with me and work with me—watch how I do it. Learn the unforced rhythms of grace. I won't lay anything heavy or ill-fitting on you. Keep company with me and you'll learn to live freely and lightly.'

Our true identity, value, worth and purpose are only really discoverable *in Christ*. This is not only true for how we understand ourselves, it is also true in so far as Christ is also our example, our source and our inspiration. His offer of restoration and renewal is to all people who will turn to Him, from the poorest of the poor to the weakest of the weak (Isa. 14:30). The beautiful reality is that Jesus looks for those who are exhausted. He comes to us when we are in the darkest and most dangerous of places and rescues us if we will only let Him (Ezek. 34:11–16). His ultimate purpose is to completely restore and renew us (1 Pet. 5:10–11).

It is little wonder then that as we experience God's restoring touch in our lives we declare that He is our salvation, our strength and our hope (Psa. 62). There have been many times when I have thought I could not go on. I have been on the brink of giving up, but God in His tenderness and mercy has sustained me and strengthened me. He has proven His faithfulness to me despite my bad decisions and my wrong patterns of work. I do not take that grace for granted but I am deeply grateful for it.

God knows where you are today. He knows how tired you can become. He is not a hard task master. He wants to restore you and give you strength. The question is whether you will let Him do it or not. Do not be afraid to stop.

Discussion Starters

1. Do you have a tendency to over-work? Where do you think that comes from?

   _____

   _____

   _____

   _____

   _____

2. Some people think that you can only get exhausted when you are doing more than God asks, but do you think it is possible to become weary in God's service? Did Jesus or the leaders of the Early Church ever show signs of exhaustion?

   _____

   _____

   _____

   _____

   _____

3. Have you ever been exhausted? If you have, what were the causes of that exhaustion?

   _____

   _____

   _____

   _____

   _____

4. Jesus invites His disciples to come to Him and experience rest. Is this your experience as a Christian? If it is not, then what do you think is wrong with the way we do Christian service and Christian community?

   _____

   _____

   _____

   _____

   _____

5. Have you tried different ways of making sure you remain connected to Jesus? Which ways worked for you and which ways did not?

_____
_____
_____
_____
_____

6. The Bible tells us that God rested on the seventh day of creation. Why did God rest and what lessons can we learn from His example?

_____
_____
_____
_____
_____

7. Discuss the principle of Sabbath – a day of restoration and renewal each week. Do you practice this principle? Jesus is described as a better Sabbath-rest for the people of God in Hebrews 4. What do you think this means?

_____
_____Heb 3 , 4_____
_____
_____
_____

8. What practical changes can you incorporate into your routine to help you rest and enjoy God's restorative work in your life?

_____
_____
_____
_____
_____

Final Thoughts

When God rested on the seventh day of creation, He did so because He was satisfied not because He was exhausted. Yet we often wait to rest until we are exhausted. True rest flows from the well of satisfaction in God.

It is possible to have a busy and full life yet to be sustained and strengthened in that life because you are deeply rooted in God and in His strength. It is also possible to live a life where you do not do a great deal but feel very drained all the time. Sometimes this is just a matter of our physical make up, but it can also be a result of having our roots in the wrong place.

People often ask me how I manage to sustain my own working/living pattern. My answer is very simple. Although the external rhythm of my life is at times quite fast, the internal rhythm of my life is very slow. I have a very determined and disciplined approach to spending time with God in prayer and praise each day. I remain connected to the source. He sustains me.

The source is always plentiful but our connection to Him is not always strong.

Closing Prayer

God my restorer,
root me deeply in You.
Help me to establish a pattern of drinking at Your well daily.
When I am weary, lift me up.
Help me to find my satisfaction in You.
Help me to base the pattern of my life on the Lord Jesus.
Strengthen my body, Lord.
Restore my soul, Lord.
Renew me, Lord.
Amen.

▶❚❚ Further Reflection

Hebrew spirituality sees the day as beginning in the evening when we go to bed. This means that when we rise in the morning, God has already been at work in us for several hours. Try this approach to your daily pattern for a week.

Our Guide in the Shadow of Confusion

Psalm 23:3; John 14:1-7

Warm Up

Select one person to walk from one side of the room to the other whilst they are blindfolded. Only one other person can guide them and only with their voice. Now repeat the exercise with everyone in the room making as much noise as possible. Discuss what this teaches you.

Opening Prayer

Father, thank You for Your Word, Your Spirit and Your Son. Thank You that Your Word brings light to our lives. Thank You that Your Spirit is always with us. Thank You that we see Your purposes so beautifully revealed in the Lord Jesus. Please help us to discover afresh the depth of Your commitment to guide us. Amen.

Eye Opener

Confusion sometimes leaves us feeling cornered. We can feel cornered by having to make a choice and not knowing what to do. Or maybe we have known what the right thing is to do but we have been anxious about what the consequences will be if we do it. Confusion comes in many guises. It can be as mundane as not knowing when to set a date in our diary or as paralysing as being unable to commit to a decision or a course of action. How do we avoid feeling cornered and instead walk in freedom?

Setting the Scene

As we reflect on the key passages before us from Psalm 23:3, John 14:1–7 and Hebrews 12:1–3 we will meet a God who is deeply interested in our lives. This is not the god of the deists who has made the world but then disengaged from it. Nor is this the god of those who see God as a fatalistic manipulator who has determined every single part of our lives. Instead we see a God who longs to guide us along the right paths and who wants to interact with us and engage with us in a meaningful and purposeful way.

Supremely, we see this God who longs to engage with us in the Person and the work of the Lord Jesus Christ Himself and in the work of the Holy Spirit who is sent to live in our lives permanently. We need not wonder what God is like because we see Him in the life and example of Jesus. We need not worry if God is distant because He has come to live within us so that we will always have our guide at hand.

The question is not whether God is interested enough in us to guide and help us. The question is whether we are willing to turn to Him for that help and guidance.

Bible Readings

Psalm 23:3

'He guides me along the right paths
for his name's sake.'

John 14:1–7

"'Do not let your hearts be troubled. You believe in God; believe also in me. My Father's house has many rooms; if that were not so, would I have told you that I am going there to prepare a place for you? And if I go and prepare a place for you, I will come back and take you to be with me that you also may be where I am. You know the way to the place where I am going."

Thomas said to him, "Lord, we don't know where you are going, so how can we know the way?"

Jesus answered, "I am the way and the truth and the life. No one comes to the Father except through me. If you really know me, you will know my Father as well. From now on, you do know him and have seen him.'"

Hebrews 12:1–3

'Therefore, since we are surrounded by such a great cloud of witnesses, let us throw off everything that hinders and the sin that so easily entangles. And let us run with

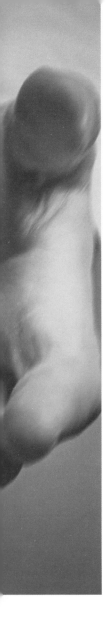

perseverance the race marked out for us, fixing our eyes on Jesus, the pioneer and perfecter of faith. For the joy that was set before him he endured the cross, scorning its shame, and sat down at the right hand of the throne of God. Consider him who endured such opposition from sinners, so that you will not grow weary and lose heart.'

John 6:68
'Lord, to whom shall we go? You have the words of eternal life.'

Exodus 15:13
'In your unfailing love you will lead
the people you have redeemed.
In your strength you will guide them
to your holy dwelling.'

Psalm 48:14
'For this God is our God for ever and ever;
he will be our guide even to the end.'

Psalm 139:7–10
'Where can I go from your Spirit?
Where can I flee from your presence?
If I go up to the heavens, you are there;
if I make my bed in the depths, you are there.
If I rise on the wings of the dawn,
if I settle on the far side of the sea,
even there your hand will guide me,
your right hand will hold me fast.'

Proverbs 3:5–6
'Trust in the Lord with all your heart
and lean not on your own understanding;
in all your ways submit to him,
and he will make your paths straight.'

Session Focus

Sometimes it is hard to make the right decision. When I was eighteen years old I had to decide whether I wanted to be a pastor or a lawyer. My family all wanted me to be a lawyer but I felt God was calling me to be a pastor. I made the hard decision to leave my law degree and pursue this calling. I believe I made the right choice but it was a very hard one because neither vocation is bad. My family took a very long time to accept my decision and it caused a great deal of pain. I believe God was guiding my decisions because He promises to lead us in the paths of righteousness (Psa. 23:3, ESV).

The truth is that God is more willing to guide us than we are to seek His guidance. I have discovered that when I make a decision then ask God to bless what I am doing, I am far more likely to end up in a bit of a mess than I am if I make a fundamental shift in my thinking so that I begin with God. If I begin with God and ask Him to help me to do what He is blessing, I am far more likely to be in a place that reflects His priorities rather than mine. I would really like to say that I always have a clear desire to do God's will rather than my own, but that is not true. Sometimes I actually fall into the trap of thinking that I have a better plan for my life than God does. That could not be further from the truth.

Self-reliance casts a shadow over our lives in so many ways. It causes us to place our reason above revelation. It makes us rely on our own ingenuity and ability rather than trust God. It puts us in the driver seat and God in the passenger seat of our lives. It gives us the prominence and not God.

The psalmist is convinced of God's readiness to lead him in God's paths of righteousness for the sake of God's own name. In other words, God's leading in our lives brings glory to God's name and reputation. To be led in the paths of righteousness is to be led in the ways of God. It is to be shown how to live a life that reflects the character, heart and love of God to the world around us. To be led in the paths of righteousness is to seek God's ways above our own because His glory matters to us more than our own glory does.

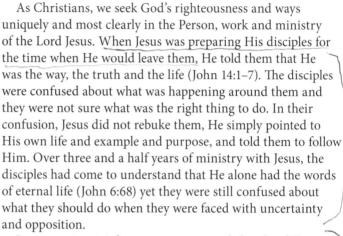

As Christians, we seek God's righteousness and ways uniquely and most clearly in the Person, work and ministry of the Lord Jesus. When Jesus was preparing His disciples for the time when He would leave them, He told them that He was the way, the truth and the life (John 14:1–7). The disciples were confused about what was happening around them and they were not sure what was the right thing to do. In their confusion, Jesus did not rebuke them, He simply pointed to His own life and example and purpose, and told them to follow Him. Over three and a half years of ministry with Jesus, the disciples had come to understand that He alone had the words of eternal life (John 6:68) yet they were still confused about what they should do when they were faced with uncertainty and opposition.

In our society it is becoming increasingly hard to follow Christ. Jesus does not fit into the culture today any more than He fitted into His own culture. His society rejected Him just as our society rejects Him. If we want to know how to live well today, then Jesus is our example. He has shown His love to us by the cross (Heb. 12:1–3). God's fundamental character has not changed and His will is made clear in His Word and in His willingness to lead His people (Exod. 15:13; Psa. 48:14). God knows what you and I are facing today. None of our dilemmas take Him by surprise (Psa. 139:7–10).

Discussion Starters

1. Do you find it easy or difficult to discern God's will? Can you explain why?

_____

_____

_____

_____

_____

2. Has there ever been a time when you have stepped out of God's will? How do you know you did this and what lessons did this teach you?

_____ Slow in obey (Turkey) _____
_____
_____
_____
_____

3. How do you think the will of God works? Does He only have one way for you to travel or does He offer you choices?

_____
_____
_____
_____
_____

4. What do you think the psalmist means when he talks about being guided in the paths of righteousness? Are there specific areas in our society that you think can lead us away from the right path?

_____
_____
_____
_____
_____

5. How do you discover the will of God for your life?

_____
_____
_____
_____
_____

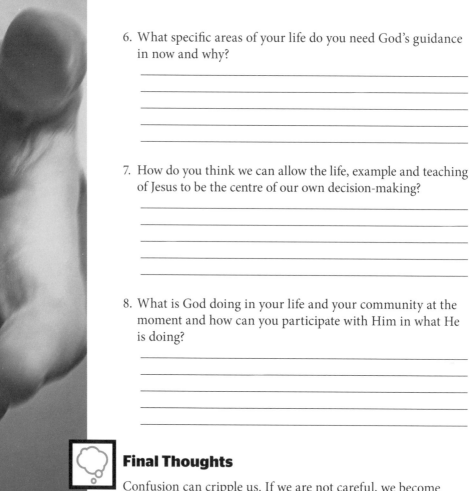

6. What specific areas of your life do you need God's guidance in now and why?

_____

_____

_____

_____

_____

7. How do you think we can allow the life, example and teaching of Jesus to be the centre of our own decision-making?

_____

_____

_____

_____

_____

8. What is God doing in your life and your community at the moment and how can you participate with Him in what He is doing?

_____

_____

_____

_____

_____

Final Thoughts

Confusion can cripple us. If we are not careful, we become trapped by the fear of making the wrong choice. What if God has more than one choice for us to make though? What if, instead of our whole lives being mapped out before us, God offers us the opportunity to make choices yet still assures us that He will finish the work He began in us?

Perhaps it is more important to have the right motivation and the right intent than it is to always be sure that you are absolutely right about a specific decision. I am not suggesting that you can do whatever you want and God will bless it. I mean that God sees your heart and is more concerned that your heart is set to do His will and your intention is to follow Him (Prov. 3:5–6). God, in His sovereignty, knows the choices you will make and has chosen to give you the freedom to make them, but at the same time He has invited you to put Him at the centre of your decision making. By doing the latter you discover a freedom in making choices that is not there if you are making them without listening to God.

Closing Prayer

God of guidance,
keep my heart set on You.
Keep my spirit tuned to the music of heaven.
Please write straight with my crooked lines.
Help me to seek Your will and Your kingdom only.
Guard me from making decisions based on self-interest.
Help me to do what You are blessing today and always.
For the glory of Your name.
Amen.

Further Reflection

Discerning the will of God can be compared to sailing in three different kinds of boat. The first is a motor boat, with God as the motor and you as a passenger. In the motor boat you are just along for the ride.

The second is a rowing boat, with you as the rower. The rowing boat is the exact opposite of the motor boat – you are in full control of where the boat goes, regardless of where God might be trying to lead you.

The third is a sailing boat, with God as the wind and you controlling the sails. In the sailing boat you can choose which way to turn the sails, either toward or away from God's direction.

Which best reflects your understanding of God's will, and why?

Our Companion in the Shadow of Despair

Psalm 23:4; John 11:21-26

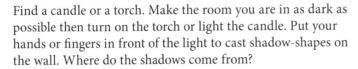

Warm Up

Find a candle or a torch. Make the room you are in as dark as possible then turn on the torch or light the candle. Put your hands or fingers in front of the light to cast shadow-shapes on the wall. Where do the shadows come from?

Opening Prayer

Father, thank You that You understand despair far more than we can understand. As we approach this subject, please walk gently with us. You know the depth of despair that touches our lives and how devastating it can be. Please open our eyes to see that You are always with us and that shadows only exist where light is. Comfort and strengthen us by Your grace. Amen.

Eye Opener

Despair can be suffocating. Whether it is caused by facing death, depression or disease, we can find our lives plummeted into a deep and dark valley without any notice and without any visible means of escape. The deeper the valley, the darker the path seems to be ahead of us and the more isolated, heartbroken and abandoned we can feel. Yet God has promised that we are never alone. What do we do when the truths we believe about God's presence do not match the experience of our lives? Where is God when life seems too painful to carry on?

Setting the Scene

There can be few more moving passages in the Bible than Psalm 23:4, the story of the resurrection of Lazarus in John 11 and Paul's powerful words about resurrection in 1 Corinthians 15. All of these feature in our Bible readings during this fourth study.

It could be argued that no words are more comforting to Christians than those we find in Scripture concerning how God has dealt with death. The selection of passages we are reflecting on reverberate with hope and burst with life. They not only speak into actual death itself, they also speak into the more general issue of despair. The words of Scripture invite us to trust in God at these times – no matter how we feel.

As we walk through life, death and despair are inevitable interlopers. The way in which we handle them demonstrates what sits at the centre of our lives. If death or despair threaten to overwhelm us, then the Bible offers us hope. Hope of a different centre, or a stronger light that can penetrate even these dark places and periods in our lives. The Bible does not leave us groping around in the dark for something to cling to when everything else has been lost. Instead, God offers us strong words of hope and sustaining power at the very worst moments of our lives.

Bible Readings

Psalm 23:4
'Even though I walk
through the darkest valley,
I will fear no evil,
for you are with me;
your rod and your staff,
they comfort me.'

John 11:21–26
"'Lord," Martha said to Jesus, "if you had been here, my brother would not have died. But I know that even now God will give you whatever you ask."

Jesus said to her, "Your brother will rise again."

Martha answered, "I know he will rise again in the resurrection at the last day."

Jesus said to her, "I am the resurrection and the life. The one who believes in me will live, even though they die; and whoever lives by believing in me will never die. Do you believe this?"'

1 Corinthians 15:54–58

'When the perishable has been clothed with the imperishable, and the mortal with immortality, then the saying that is written will come true: "Death has been swallowed up in victory."

"Where, O death, is your victory?

Where, O death, is your sting?"

The sting of death is sin, and the power of sin is the law. But thanks be to God! He gives us the victory through our Lord Jesus Christ.

Therefore, my dear brothers and sisters, stand firm. Let nothing move you. Always give yourselves fully to the work of the Lord, because you know that your labour in the Lord is not in vain.'

Revelation 21:4

'"He will wipe every tear from their eyes. There will be no more death" or mourning or crying or pain, for the old order of things has passed away.'

Psalm 3:5–6

'I lie down and sleep;

I wake again, because the LORD sustains me.

I will not fear though tens of thousands assail me on every side.'

Psalm 27:1

'The LORD is my light and my salvation –

whom shall I fear?

The LORD is the stronghold of my life –

of whom shall I be afraid?'

1 Peter 1:3–6

'Praise be to the God and Father of our Lord Jesus Christ! In his great mercy he has given us new birth into a living hope through the resurrection of Jesus Christ from the dead, and into an inheritance that can never perish, spoil or fade. This inheritance is kept in heaven for you, who through faith are shielded by God's power until the coming of the salvation that is ready to be revealed in the last time. In all this you greatly rejoice, though now for a little while you may have had to suffer grief in all kinds of trials.'

Session Focus

We were not made for death – we were made for life. When death intrudes upon our lives, therefore, we hate it. Of all the shadows we have explored: confusion, worry and exhaustion, death is by far the darkest. It lingers over us and threatens to destroy our hope and steal away our faith. Or perhaps it has only done that to me.

In August 2002 my father dropped dead. I was devastated but slowly recovered a sense of God's grace and comfort. In July 2014 my eldest brother's partner committed suicide. In November 2014 my sister's only son committed suicide. In April 2015 my sister's husband, heartbroken at the loss of their son, also took his own life. I cannot begin to explain the nuclear devastation these deaths have caused in our family. We have survived, and in many ways are stronger but the tragedies have been some of the darkest and saddest days I have ever experienced. To see my family carry such despair has been almost unbearable. At times I have thought that the shadow of death was a permanent darkness. Yet in the midst of this darkness, I have known a light that has shone on the path in front of me. I have known that even the shadow of death is not a permanent feature of my life. Death's companion, despair, has tried to suffocate me but it has not succeeded. Its icy cold hands have been loosened from my neck by God Himself. He will not let despair or death destroy me.

Psalm 23:4 has carried me through these dark days. The psalmist is very clear, God is present even in the very darkest valley. Nothing is able to destroy His presence. This conviction has given me hope, moment by moment, in these dark and sorrowful days, along with Jesus' actions at the death of His friend, Lazarus (John 11).

Jesus allowed His friend Lazarus to die. When Lazarus'

sisters, Mary and Martha, sent a message to Jesus asking Him to come and help, Jesus deliberately stayed away and waited until Lazarus was dead. You can hear Martha's disappointment when she says to Jesus, 'If you had been here ...' I know what that feels like. When my nephew and brother-in-law died, I placed my hands on their heads and asked God to resurrect them – He didn't do it. I still wish He had.

So how does Jesus' claim to be the resurrection and the life make sense (John 11:21–26)? Why did He let Mary and Martha weep when He knew that in a few moments He would bring their brother back from the dead? I think Jesus was redeeming the darkness of grief. He was giving Mary and Martha, and by extension us, permission to grieve when we lose those we love. He was going further though; by allowing His friend to die, Jesus was pointing to someone other than Himself and showing that He had power over death itself. The only way He could do that was by letting Lazarus die, then bringing him back.

Lazarus' death did not end in death. Christ conquered death for Lazarus, then by going to the cross and dying Himself, Christ has conquered death for all of us. The dark shadow of death is destroyed by the brilliance of Christ's resurrection. Lazarus' resurrection is proof of Christ's power to raise the dead. Christ's resurrection is proof of Christ's ultimate power over death itself. In defeating death, Christ has defeated sin. Therefore, neither hold power over Christians any longer (1 Cor. 15:54–58).

I am utterly convinced that death has not had the last word because death itself has been defeated. The greatest fear of the human heart has been dissolved by Christ's own death and resurrection (Heb. 2:14). That is why I can sleep in peace at night (Psa. 3:5–6). It is why my ultimate fear has been destroyed (Psa. 27:1) and I therefore have hope: the deep hope of heaven (1 Pet. 1:3–6), and the reality that God will wipe away every tear. That death itself will be no more means that even in the darkest, deepest valley there is hope.

God is with us even in the darkness of death. Death is but a fleeting shadow.

Discussion Starters

1. Have you lost someone you love? What impact has it had on your faith?

   _____

   _____

   _____

   _____

2. In what ways have you experienced the comfort and the presence of God in the midst of death and despair?

   _____

   _____

   _____

   _____

3. Psalm 84:6 describes walking through the Valley of Baka (which means 'tears') and making a spring there. Are there ways in which you have discovered something new about God's character in times of despair and sadness?

   _____You_far_a_spring_____

   _____for_others_to_drink_o_____

   _____be_comforted_____

   _____

4. Reflect on the story of the resurrection of Lazarus. Why do you think Jesus wept at the graveside of Lazarus?

   _____

   _____

   _____

   _____

5. In what ways do you think Jesus redeems grief for us by letting Martha and Mary grieve? Do you think that was cruel?

   _____

   _____

   _____

   _____

6. Reflect on the idea that we were not made for death and so that is why we hate it. Do you think there is a difference between the fear of death and the fear of dying itself?

_____

_____

_____

_____

7. Do you know anyone who is currently going through the shadow of death? Take a few moments to pray for them now.

_____

_____

_____

_____

8. How can your church support those who are grieving? Is there a way your group could help someone who is struggling with loss?

_____

_____

_____

_____

Final Thoughts

I wrote this poem after the death of my friend, Peter Bond. I miss him very much. Use it as a reflection as you think about the victory of Christ in resurrection.

For Peter
What victory, death, can you claim over him?
A crumpled body all that remains
for you to say you 'won'
and even that will one day yield
a glorious new beginning ...

But know this – you do not conquer him.
He broke your grip and is more fully alive
than he has ever been.

He is more beautifully himself now
and forever stands beyond your paltry reach.

His last breath a cry of 'finished' faith
Things once unseen, now seen,
Things once imagined, now before him,
Whilst you remain in dark corners
he sings of hope with glinting eye.

Looking to the One who made it possible
Whilst you, you are nothing more than a distant memory
Of a doorway into glory.
Who won this battle?
I tell you he did, for he stands in the victory of his Victor.

Closing Prayer

Resurrected Lord,
we were not made for death.
Help us not to be afraid of death.
When we do not sense or see You,
give us the assurance that You are there.
A day is coming when death itself will be destroyed.
Give us grace and courage to trust You,
and help us live in the power of Your resurrection.
Amen.

Further Reflection

Shadows can only exist where a light is present. John's Gospel
opens with this brilliant truth: darkness cannot overcome the
light (John 1:3–5). Look at various translations of those verses
and then light a candle; as you watch it burn reflect on the
power of Christ in your life.

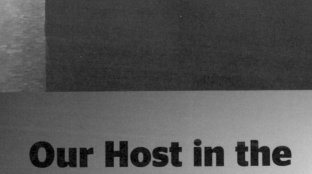

Our Host in the Shadow of Attack

Psalm 23:5; John 6:26-35, 41, 48, 51

Warm Up

Have you ever been invited to a friend's house for dinner or invited someone to your home for a meal? What is it about sharing a meal with someone that is so special? Why does it feel particularly helpful when you are going through a hard time?

Opening Prayer

Father, thank You for being our defender. In the midst of our battles, please remind us of Your strength, commitment and love for us. As we think about those areas of our lives where we need You most, we ask You to give us the grace to see things through Your eyes. Help us to lean into Your strength, remembering that it is always available for us. Amen.

Eye Opener

There are times when we cry out, 'Lord, when is this going to end?' Battle-weary and worn down, everything seems to be going wrong and no one seems to be able to help us. These seasons can last a long time and can leave us feeling vulnerable, bruised and confused. Attacks and criticisms at work, problems in our families and relationships, and the whispers of our old enemy, Satan, leave us feeling very exposed. What we need most is a sense of God being on our side. Where does that come from and how do we maintain it?

Setting the Scene

On first reading, it might feel like the scriptures we are exploring together in this study are disconnected. What do Jesus' statements that He is the bread of life (John 6) have to do with the declaration that God prepares a table for the psalmist in the presence of his enemies (Psa. 23:5)? The link is that for the psalmist, God has become his host – his sustainer and provider at the moments in his life when he is most at threat and in the greatest danger.

Jesus has become our host. He is the One who welcomes us to His table, to eat bread and drink wine on a regular basis to remember what He has done for us. Yet He is more than just inviting us to a meal to remember Him. His work on the cross is the very 'meat and drink' of Christian faith. It is in His life, death and resurrection that we find our greatest victory. It is in Him that our salvation and our hope is secured. It is in Him that we find life and sustenance because Jesus Himself is our sustainer and our provider.

The Bible readings we are focusing on remind us of our constant need to rely on God's grace and mercy, shown to us in Jesus and offered to us through Christ.

Bible Readings

Psalm 23:5
'You prepare a table before me
in the presence of my enemies.
You anoint my head with oil;
my cup overflows.'

John 6:26–35,41,48,51
'Jesus answered, "Very truly I tell you, you are looking for me, not because you saw the signs I performed but because you ate the loaves and had your fill. Do not work for food that spoils, but for food that endures to eternal life, which the Son of Man will give you. For on him God the Father has placed his seal of approval."

Then they asked him, "What must we do to do the works God requires?"

Jesus answered, "The work of God is this: to believe in the one he has sent."

So they asked him, "What sign then will you give that we may see it and believe you? What will you do? Our ancestors ate the manna in the wilderness; as it is written: 'He gave them bread from heaven to eat.'"

Jesus said to them, "Very truly I tell you, it is not Moses who has given you the bread from heaven, but it is my

Father who gives you the true bread from heaven. For the bread of God is the bread that comes down from heaven and gives life to the world."

"Sir," they said, "always give us this bread."

Then Jesus declared, "I am the bread of life. Whoever comes to me will never go hungry, and whoever believes in me will never be thirsty."

41 ... "I am the bread that came down from heaven."

48 ... "I am the bread of life."

51 ... "I am the living bread that came down from heaven. Whoever eats this bread will live for ever. This bread is my flesh, which I will give for the life of the world.'"

1 John 2:20,27

'But you have an anointing from the Holy One, and all of you know the truth ... As for you, the anointing you received from him remains in you, and you do not need anyone to teach you. But as his anointing teaches you about all things and as that anointing is real, not counterfeit – just as it has taught you, remain in him.'

Psalm 16:5

'LORD, you alone are my portion and my cup;
you make my lot secure.'

Psalm 116:13

'I will lift up the cup of salvation
and call on the name of the LORD.'

Session Focus

Who or what we run to when we are under attack reveals where our trust lies. The thing that we most hunger for is the thing that we will seek most diligently.

I know a young man who for many years sought the approval of others. He was desperate to be seen to be successful. He needed to be needed so much that he was driven by an insatiable desire to be affirmed and approved by others.

Throughout his whole life he had thought he was useless. Someone he loved had always thought him stupid and he was constantly blamed for the problems in his home. He felt terrible about himself and as a result sought value and worth in what others thought of him. He was always running away from negative views of himself. Then he met Jesus and his life was utterly transformed. He discovered that God loved him, valued him and welcomed him with open arms. God set a place at the table for that young man. The young man now knows that he is secure in God's love.

The psalmist cries out that God has prepared a table for him in the presence of his enemies (Psa. 23:5). After feeling threatened, insecure and isolated, the psalmist now finds peace, security and comfort in God. Not only that, but God also anoints his head with oil. That is a picture of acceptance, adoption and inclusion into the royal household. The psalmist is welcome in God's company and safe in God's care. He has found a place to be – a place to belong. He has found a home.

This is a picture of what God does for all who come to Him. We so often look in the wrong places for acceptance and value and worth. We seek security in the wrong things. Causal sexual encounters, the amount of money in our bank accounts, the titles we hold or the cars we drive. We are people on the run, desperately looking for security and someone to show us that we matter, when all the time God is holding open the doors of His home to us and inviting us in.

Only God can defend us against the onslaught of our enemies (Psa. 16:5). Only God can provide us with safety. Jesus, in a dialogue with religious leaders, describes Himself as the bread of life (John 6:35,41,48,51). As the bread of life He is the One who sustains us as we believe in Him. He is greater than Moses because He not only provides access to God's sustenance, Jesus Himself is that sustenance. He describes Himself as living bread, as the bread that has come down from heaven, and He invites those who are willing to partake of His body and His life. His invitation is an open one. He says *whoever* comes will never go hungry and *whoever* believes will never thirst.

There are many things that attack us: our own insecurities, other people's views of us, our past, our mistakes, our pride and our arrogance. There is only one place, however, where we find shelter from all of these attackers: in God Himself. He has already prepared a table for us. He has made a way. He does not promise to remove us from the challenges that we face, rather He promises to prepare a table for us in the presence of our enemies. What a powerful thought.

How does God prepare such a table for us? By enduing us with the abiding power and presence of the Holy Spirit, He stands with us, around us and in us. In 1 John 2:20,27 John tells his readers that God has given them an anointing that is permanent and present. That anointing will guard and guide them if they will let it. It seems clear to me that the promises of Jesus in John 14–16, about the work and ministry of the Holy Spirit, are deeply reassuring for those of us who need to know that God is always with us. We carry God's presence, God's anointing, simply because we are Christians. Indeed, the word *Christ* itself means *anointed One*, and the word *Christian* means we belong to the anointed One – we are part of His household and His family; the household of the anointed, the family of the anointed.

Whatever enemies I may face, real or imagined, God is with me. Always.

Discussion Starters

1. What are the enemies that you think threaten your identity in Christ?

   _____

   _____

   _____

   _____

   _____

2. What do you run to for security?

Pray

3. What do you most hunger for and how is that hunger evidenced in your life?

4. Many Christians believe that God will not let them suffer, yet the reality is that Christians do suffer. How does the reality that God is with us when we suffer or face attack help us?

5. Have you ever sensed God's presence with you in a particular situation?

In big things like China, Romania etc
In little things (looke after the birds)

6. How does the presence of God help you deal with what you are facing?

_____

_____

_____

_____

_____

7. Do you ever wonder where God is? What do you do in those times?

_____

_____

_____

_____

_____

8. How can you be a support and a help for someone else who needs to know God's love for them and His heart towards them at the moment?

_____

_____

_____

_____

_____

Final Thoughts

There are times when we do not have the strength to do very much. In those moments in my own life I have found great strength and great comfort in Holy Communion.

The bread and wine are each a symbol. The bread represents Christ's body that was broken for me and the wine represents His blood that was shed for me. In my moments of utter weakness, as I eat the bread and drink the wine, God pours His strength into my life. Whereas the psalmist in Psalm 23 talks about God preparing a table for him in the presence of his enemies, for us, Christ has become the very host. He not only provides the table, He is the meal. To eat the bread and drink the wine is to enter into the mystery of Christ's suffering in a powerful way, and to remember the death of Christ and what He has done for us in an act of simple faith, by believing that God is powerfully present. Something more than just bread and wine is received as we eat. Grace is bestowed upon us in a special way. All we need to do is open our mouths in faith and God will feed us, sustain us and anoint us afresh.

Closing Prayer

Bread of life,
we hunger for You.
You alone can satisfy our deepest needs.
You alone bring us security.
Forgive us when we run to the wrong things
for protection or for nourishment.
As we come to You, give us faith to believe
that You are all we need.
Sustain us moment by moment
and continually anoint us with Your presence.
Amen.

Further Reflection

What does it mean to eat the bread of life? Somehow, it means identifying with the Lord Jesus. It means to follow Him. Are you willing to do this? As you approach Holy Week, how can you carry your cross?

Our Peace in the Shadow of Tomorrow

Psalm 23:6; John 8:12; 9:5; 15:1,5

Warm Up

Imagine you are looking down into a canyon where all of your worries and anxieties are. Now imagine that instead of looking down, you look up and discover God is holding you securely like a great eagle. How does the change in perspective make you feel? What lessons do you learn?

Opening Prayer

Father, thank You that You know tomorrow before it begins. You know the end from the beginning. Please bring to our attention those areas of our lives where we need to learn to trust You more and worry less. Thank You that You are more committed to us than we are to You. Thank You that You live in us by the power of the Holy Spirit. Amen.

Eye Opener

Being afraid of the future is a killer. It kills joy, peace, hope, faith and assurance. Fear and faith do not sit well together. Fear is rooted in uncertainty about God's faithfulness. Faith is rooted in certainty about God's faithfulness. The challenge for many of us is that we can be so caught up in the 'what if' scenarios of our lives that we lose sight of one of the crucial elements of Christian faith: God holds on to us, we do not hold on to Him. We are not pursuing God. God is pursuing us.

Setting the Scene

Our Bible readings for this final study remind us that God is the central character in the drama of our lives and not us. We can often take on the role of the hero, inviting God to respond to our decisions and our actions. This is not the role He wants to play! Instead, God is the main character in the drama of time and history, and He is the main character in each of our lives. Our readings remind us of this reality.

The last verse of Psalm 23 reminds us that God pursues us, we do not pursue Him. God has taken the initiative. He has come to us as the light of the world (John 8:12; 9:5) and the vine from whom we gain life, and without Him we can do nothing (John 15:1,5). Christ is the provider of all that we need for godly living (2 Peter 1:3–4).

The great danger of how we understand Christianity is that we allow ourselves to think that God has saved us by grace and the rest is up to us. This leads to a works-based pursuit of God, which can never satisfy us. The biblical reality is that God has pursued us. He came to us. He has revealed Himself to us. The great paradox of Christian faith is that the One whom we pursue is the pursuer Himself.

 ## Bible Readings

Psalm 23:6

'Surely your goodness and love will follow me
all the days of my life,
and I will dwell in the house of the LORD
for ever.'

John 8:12; 9:5

'When Jesus spoke again to the people, he said, "I am the light of the world. Whoever follows me will never walk in darkness, but will have the light of life."

… "While I am in the world, I am the light of the world.'"

John 14:25–27

'All this I have spoken while still with you. But the Advocate, the Holy Spirit, whom the Father will send in my name, will teach you all things and will remind you of everything I have said to you. Peace I leave with you; my peace I give you. I do not give to you as the world gives. Do not let your hearts be troubled and do not be afraid.'

John 15:1,5

'I am the true vine, and my Father is the gardener … you are the branches. If you remain in me and I in you, you will bear much fruit; apart from me you can do nothing.'

2 Peter 1:3–4

'His divine power has given us everything we need for a godly life through our knowledge of him who called us by his own glory and goodness. Through these he has given us his very great and precious promises, so that through them you may participate in the divine nature, having escaped the corruption in the world caused by evil desires.'

Psalm 43:3

'Send me your light and your faithful care,
let them lead me;
let them bring me to your holy mountain,
to the place where you dwell.'

Psalm 79:8

'Do not hold against us the sins of past generations;
may your mercy come quickly to meet us,
for we are in desperate need.'

Psalm 89:14

'Righteousness and justice are the foundation of your throne;
love and faithfulness go before you.'

Ephesians 2:14–18

'For he himself is our peace, who has made the two groups one and has destroyed the barrier, the dividing wall of hostility, by setting aside in his flesh the law with its commands and regulations. His purpose was to create in himself one new humanity out of the two, thus making peace, and in one body to reconcile both of them to God through the cross, by which he put to death their hostility. He came and preached peace to you who were far away and peace to those who were near. For through him we both have access to the Father by one Spirit.'

Colossians 3:15

'Let the peace of Christ rule in your hearts, since as members of one body you were called to peace. And be thankful.'

2 Thessalonians 3:16

'Now may the Lord of peace himself give you peace at all times and in every way. The Lord be with all of you.'

Session Focus

There is no uncertainty in God's commitment to us. He relentlessly pursues us with His goodness and His mercy. He is far more committed to us than we are to Him (Psa. 23:6).

I have let God down many, many times. If I had the opportunity to live my life again, there are many things I would not do. That is not to say that I live with deep regrets. Instead, I recognise my brokenness and my fallen nature and the weakness of my passion and commitment to Christ. I may have failed Him many times but the life-transforming reality is that God has never let me down, and He never will. We began our Lent studies looking at the God who is our shepherd in the shadow of today. We end our studies reflecting on the God who is our deep peace in the shadow of tomorrow.

God promises to carry us across the finishing line of faith. His goodness and His love will sustain and guard us. In the middle of Psalm 23 we read of God's rod and staff comforting us. At the end of the psalm we see His goodness personified, pursuing us.

None of us knows what tomorrow will hold. As I write these words, I am awaiting the passing into eternity of a number of people in my congregation and my own mum. She is slowly weakening. At the same time, my wife has struggled with ill health for many years. One of our sons lived for twenty years with a very debilitating condition. We learnt many years ago that if we worried about the future, we would never be able to enjoy the gift of the present. There are many aspects of our lives over which we have no control but we can choose to keep our gaze set on God and allow Him to be our peace and our hope. God pursues us with an intensity of love and passion that is unimaginable to us and indescribable. He loves us so deeply and He longs for us to be humble enough to confess our need of Him. He will lead us and guide us and bring us home to Himself if we will only ask Him (Psa. 43:3). If we are humble enough to confess our need of Him, He is ready to scoop us up and carry us home (Psa. 79:8).

Jesus is the light that we need to navigate tomorrow; He will not let us down (John 8:12; 9:5). In the midst of all our religious service and acts of worship, it is life-giving to remember that in Christ we have all we need for godly living (2 Pet. 1:3–4). He is our peace (Eph. 2:14–18; Col. 3:15).

In Psalm 23 we are told that we will dwell in His house forever. The New Testament not only affirms the reality that one day we will be with Him forever but it also elaborates this truth, reminding us that God has come to dwell in us. God, our relentless pursuer, has come to take up residence in us and we now find our home in God Himself, not just in the environment where God is.

Whatever shadows try to hide the light from our lives, they cannot conceal Him precisely because He will finish the work He has begun in us (Phil. 1:6). Nothing can separate us from the love of God in Christ (Rom. 8:31–39). It does not matter whether the fleeting shadows are worry, exhaustion, confusion, death and despair, attacks or fear of the unknown, God is utterly committed to us.

As we approach Holy Week, we will remember just how committed God is. As we walk the Via Dolorosa and stand at the foot of Golgotha's mound, my prayer is that we will see the extent of God's love. The world went dark as the Saviour died but that darkness was broken. Resurrection Morning will see the sun rise and we will remember that all shadows are fleeting. They will all give way to the light of Christ one day. This is our great hope. This is what fills us with peace (2 Thess. 3:16).

Discussion Starters

1. In what ways do you think we over-emphasise our pursuit of God and under-emphasise God's pursuit of us?

   Legalistic

2. How does it make you feel to be reminded that God is more committed to you than you are to Him?

3. Do you have any particular anxieties about the future? How does the assurance of God's goodness and peace help you face those anxieties?

4. Looking back, are there past issues or shadows that you have seen God minister into?

   big things repaly have yind Clear

   Small things.

5. Are there issues or shadows in your life now that you need God to bring change to?

_____

_____

_____

_____

_____

6. What things have you discovered about God that have brought you closer to Him?

His love, faithfulness
His perfect plan
How safe we are in Him.

7. As you prepare for Holy Week, how can you allow space and time each day to remind yourself of Christ's love for you?

_____

_____

_____

_____

_____

8. Looking ahead to Easter Sunday, how can you celebrate that the light of the world conquered the darkness on that day?

_____

_____

_____

_____

_____

Final Thoughts

Jesus declared that He is the light of the world at the height of the festival that was taking place in Jerusalem (John 8:12). In the same way, at the height of another festival He declared that He is the water of life (John 7:37–39). These two announcements were made in the midst of deep religious celebrations yet Jesus' announcements were missed by many.

Traditionally, Lent is a time when we reflect on our lives and our walk with God, and we take time to draw near to Him once again. What a shame it would be if we observed the religious festival but missed the most astounding thing of all: God has come near to us. As much as we pursue God, He pursues us more. He is not playing a game of hide and seek with us. He wants us to find Him. He wants us to encounter Him in fresh and new ways. There is more of God for us to explore. We have only just scratched the surface of His goodness and mercy.

One day, we will be bathed in His light and we will live in a land where there are no shadows at all. In the meantime, we remind ourselves that all of the shadows that invade our lives are temporary. They will all be dissolved by the radiance of our King. May He shine in your life today.

Closing Prayer

Relentless, pursuing God,
You have not given up on us.
You will complete the work You have begun in us.
One day all shadows will be removed.
Give us grace to walk in Your light.
Help us share the hope of Your life.
We worship and adore You,
the God of light and life in whom
there is no shadow of turning.
Amen.

Further Reflection

What are the three things you have been most deeply impacted by during your Lenten reflections this year? How will you allow God to use those things to draw you into a deeper relationship and encounter with Him?

Leader's Notes

General Notes

The subject matter for the study guide is simple: what are some of the things that cause shadows to fall on our lives and what light can we find in God's Word?

The studies are built around Psalm 23 and some of the 'I am' sayings of Christ in John's Gospel. These readings serve as the anchor points for each of the studies and they are augmented by various other texts from across the Scriptures. By linking the readings, I hope to demonstrate the unity of Scripture and embed the whole study in the life and ministry of Christ as we approach Lent.

The studies deal with what could be pastorally sensitive issues (particularly Study Two and Study Four), so I would encourage you to ensure that you have thought through adequate pastoral responses for each week. It is a great privilege to open up the Scriptures with people, but also a great responsibility. May God enable you to lead the studies gently and sensitively.

STUDY ONE:
Our Shepherd in the Shadow of Today

The aim of this study is to help the group think about their worries and concerns for today, yet trustfully placing them in the hands of God. To do this we will explore the role of Jesus as the shepherd. You may like to particularly highlight the following:

- The image of the shepherd was such an important one in both Israel and in the Early Church. As mentioned in the study, you might like to find, print out and show the group pictures of the earliest images of Jesus, found in the Roman catacombs, where He is depicted as the shepherd.
- The idea that when the sheep left the security of a pen or a resting place and entered into open country, they were completely and utterly dependent upon the shepherd. She or

he was the only person who could protect them against the inevitable attacks of wild animals and robbers, etc. In the same way, we are utterly and solely dependent upon God for grace and protection.

- One of the issues we face is the tension between holding on to the shepherd who protects us and still walking in a world where the shadows of life affect us. It's important to help individuals in the group acknowledge and then come to terms with this tension.

STUDY TWO:
Our Restorer in the Shadow of Exhaustion

This aim of this study is to help the group understand that Sabbath-rest is about satisfaction and not exhaustion, and we can only find our true satisfaction when we find our true identity in Christ. Here are some suggestions for leading this study and points to be aware of:

- I strongly recommend you read Eugene Peterson's paraphrase of Matthew 11:28–30 in *The Message*. Try to avoid rushing it. You might want to read it a couple of times and point out the beauty of the imagery to the group.
- There is an interesting theme of Sabbath to pick up in the study, which we cannot go into too deeply, but you may want to do some preparation by reading Hebrews 3 and 4. Christ is presented there as our better Sabbath and the idea of Sabbath-rest is an important metaphor to unpack a little bit. Christ is a better Sabbath because He was there before the Sabbath.
- You might also want to refer the group to some of the passages in the Gospels, (I think Mark's Gospel is particularly helpful here) where Jesus challenges the Pharisees and scribes in their understanding of the Sabbath. Be careful not to fall into the trap of saying Jesus broke the Sabbath as that is not true. He broke the additional expectations of the Sabbath created by successive generations of Rabbis, but He did not break the teaching of the Pentateuch.
- I'd also suggest you avoid being drawn into the red herring discussion of Sabbath day observance.

- Please be aware that many members of your group could find the application of Matthew 11 very difficult – particularly if you are part of a very busy church family. Allow the group time to think about whether they are doing too much. Picking up the ideas of rhythm and rest here will be helpful, particularly the idea of the Jewish rhythm for a day (see Further Reflection).

STUDY THREE:
Our Guide in the Shadow of Confusion

This study aims to unpack the question of choices and what to do when we face a number of good alternative choices and do not know which one to pursue. Here are some points to look out for or think about:

- A strict and narrow understanding of the will of God can actually cripple people and make them fearful about the choices they make. You probably need to allow space and time for people to discuss the various views of the will of God. Is there only one clear and decisive will of God or does He have various routes that we can take?
- Conversations about the will of God can sometimes get a little intense, so perhaps you could lighten the mood by using an example such as asking the participants if they pray about the colour of socks they should wear each day, or what milk to buy, or where to buy their shopping each month, etc.
- I have used an illustration at the end of the study about three boats – a motor boat, a rowing boat and a sailing boat. It might be helpful for the participants to think about how they need to change the direction of the sail to catch the wind (John 3 helps to point out that the Holy Spirit is a Wind that blows where He wants). Unpack the possibility that God can disrupt our plans and make us go in one direction and then another.
Are the participants comfortable with that idea? If they struggle with it, ask them if the Virgin Mary had her plans upset by God's intervention in her life.

STUDY FOUR:
Our Companion in the Shadow of Despair

The aim of this study is to reflect on the truth that death is but a fleeting shadow and that even in the darkness of death, God is with us. You might want to read the whole of John 11, although it is a very long section. There are important questions in the passage though, and things to highlight, such as:

- Why did Jesus delay and not come immediately when He heard of Lazarus' illness?
- How come the disciples seemed so confused by this whole exchange? Aren't we equally confused by death and illness?
- Why did Jesus say that Lazarus' sickness would not end in death when it clearly did? Of course it did not, because Lazarus passed through death and out the other side. He did not stay dead. The same is true for us, the only difference is the gap between our death and resurrection is longer. The other issue to highlight concerning Lazarus' resurrection, and indeed every other resurrection apart from Christ's, is that they are temporary. All those who have been resurrected die again, except of course Jesus, who is therefore the firstborn from amongst the dead.
- Why doesn't Jesus stop the tears of Mary and Martha?

This week's study is likely to be a very important one and I would encourage you to leave room for a time of prayer, perhaps breaking into twos so that individuals can express their personal prayers more freely. If you know of those who are struggling with bereavement and loss you might want to look out for them specifically.

STUDY FIVE: Our Host in the Shadow of Attack

The aim of this study is to think about where we run to when we are under attack, while encouraging us to enter into the life of Christ by following Him, identifying with Him and letting Him shape our identity. Here are some points to think about before you lead the study:

- Be careful not to allow the idea of attackers to become too narrow. I have deliberately chosen a story about a young man whose attackers were the voices from his past that made him feel inadequate and unloved. There is no doubt that some of the participants will be impacted by these truths, so once again pastoral sensitivity is really to be encouraged.
- There is a theological nuance to be wary of: the idea of the anointing in 1 John 2:20,27. As you explain this, be careful to link the idea of anointing with the power and presence of the Spirit in our lives, and with the idea that we are all 'anointed ones' – be careful not to turn the idea of anointing here into some special gift for only a few. That is another subject and you do not want to get lost in a side street!
- You may want to suggest having Communion together, either during this study or the next one.

STUDY SIX:
Our Peace in the Shadow of Tomorrow

This study serves as a summary, whilst at the same time focusing in on the idea of God being our peace and our pursuer. The aim of the study is to help the group take their attention off the things that they do to follow God and focus their minds on the many things that God does to pursue them. Here are some suggestions for this final study:

- As this study is about God pursuing us, the section that deals with the indwelling Holy Spirit is particularly important.
- It is worth unpacking 2 Peter 1:3–4 a little, encouraging the group to think about the dangers of constantly asking God for more. That's not to say that pursuing God is wrong, but sometimes we can end up with so much emphasis on us pursuing God that we lose sight of the fact that God is far more passionate about us than we are about Him.
- It might be worth picking up some images of God pursuing us in this study – perhaps the images in Luke 15.
- It's also worth allowing time for reflection, thinking back to all the studies so that people have a chance to reflect on what God has been saying to them.

- If you did not have Communion last week, you could have it this week, combining it with a time of thanksgiving, sharing what God has done.

smallGroup central

All of our small group ideas and resources in one place

Online:

www.smallgroupcentral.org.uk
is filled with free video teaching,
tools, articles and a whole host of
ideas.

On the road:

A range of seminars themed for
small groups can be brought to
your local community. Contact us at
hello@smallgroupcentral.org.uk

In print:

Books, study guides and DVDs
covering an extensive list of themes,
Bible books and life issues.

Log on and find out more at:
www.smallgroupcentral.org.uk

Courses and events

Waverley Abbey College

Publishing and media

Conference facilities

Transforming lives

CWR's vision is to enable people to experience personal transformation through applying God's Word to their lives and relationships.

Our Bible-based training and resources help people around the world to:
• Grow in their walk with God
• Understand and apply Scripture to their lives
• Resource themselves and their church
• Develop pastoral care and counselling skills
• Train for leadership
• Strengthen relationships, marriage and family life and much more.

Our insightful writers provide daily Bible-reading notes and other resources for all ages, and our experienced course designers and presenters have gained an international reputation for excellence and effectiveness.

CWR's Training and Conference Centres in Surrey and East Sussex, England, provide excellent facilities in idyllic settings – ideal for both learning and spiritual refreshment.

CWR Applying God's Word
to everyday life and relationships

CWR, Waverley Abbey House,
Waverley Lane, Farnham,
Surrey GU9 8EP, UK

Telephone: **+44 (0)1252 784700**
Email: info@cwr.org.uk
Website: www.cwr.org.uk

Registered Charity No. 294387
Company Registration No. 1990308